LA 2

W9-BAP-466

Early Reading Comprehension
in Varied Subject Matter

JANE ERVIN

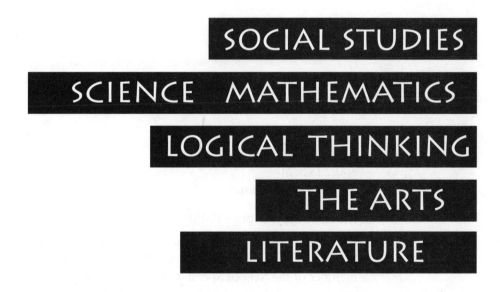

SOCIAL STUDIES

SCIENCE   MATHEMATICS

LOGICAL THINKING

THE ARTS

LITERATURE

EDUCATORS PUBLISHING SERVICE
Cambridge and Toronto

Dr. Ervin would like to thank the National Geographic Society for their interest in the development of these books, and particularly the editors of *World* magazine, whose lively, interesting articles provided a stimulating resource that contributed greatly to the quality of the selections.

Educators Publishing Service
800.225.5750
www.epsbooks.com

Illustrated by George Phillips

Copyright © 2001, 1999, 1996, 1993, 1990, 1982 by Educators Publishing Service, a division of School Specialty Publishing, a member of the School Specialty Family. All rights reserved. No part of this book may be reproduced or utilized in any form or by any electronic or mechanical means, including photocopying, without permission in writing from the publisher.

Printed in U.S.A.

978-0-8388-0621-0
7 8 9 10 11 CUR 11 10 09 08 07

CONTENTS

subject: general topics

subject: social studies

subject: science

subject: logical thinking

subject: math

subject: literature

subject: the arts

1 Night Bird

When do owls fly?

Have you ever seen an owl? Owls are birds that come out at night. You may see just two **bright** yellow eyes **staring** at you or hear a loud **hoot**.

It's not hard for owls to fly and hunt at night. They are not like most other birds. They can see well in the dark.

Owls have very good hearing, too. They can hear the sound of a rat or mouse from far off. They can fly right to it.

Owls make very little noise when they fly. They can **surprise** the little animals they eat.

The passage is about

   (a) eagles   (b) robins   ⓒ owls

Can you remember?

1. When do owls hunt?

   (a) daytime   ⓑ nighttime   (c) both day and night

2. What can owls do that other birds cannot do? They can

   (a) fly very high   (b) walk   ⓒ see well in the dark

3. Owls like to eat

(a) mice   (b) flies   (c) plants

4. Owls can surprise an animal because

(a) they hide in trees   (b) they creep on the   (c) their wings don't
                               ground   make much noise

5. Do owls find it easy to hunt in the dark?

(a) yes   (b) no   (c) can't say

Put the sentences in the correct order.

__3__ Owls can hear well, too.

__4__ Owls make very little noise when they fly.

__2__ It's not hard for owls to fly and hunt at night.

__1__ Have you ever seen an owl?

Match the words with their meanings.

__c__ 1. bright   (a) to come upon without warning

__d__ 2. staring   (b) sound made by an owl

__b__ 3. hoot   (c) shining

__a__ 4. surprise   (d) looking hard, for a long time

Write about it.

1. Write 2 sentences about the same subject. Use 1 of the words from "Match the words with their meanings."

2. Using your own words, write 3 things you have learned about owls from the story you just read.

2 Trees on the Move

How do trees get planted?

Do you ever think about where all the trees around us come from? People **plant** some, but most trees get there in other ways.

Trees begin as **tiny** seeds. The wind and rain take the seeds into the air and carry them far and wide. Some **float** down streams and rivers. Some fall on animals' fur and drop off as the animals move about. Some are eaten by birds and **scattered** in their droppings. Sometimes seeds fall on the ground and just roll along. Sometimes they fall on us, and we **spread** them around as we move. When they get to the ground, some of them will take root.

The passage is about

   (a) kinds of trees   (b) how trees get   (c) how to look after
                         planted   a tree

Can you remember?

1. Which of these can help plant a tree?
   (a) a bird   (b) a cat   (c) a clock

2. Trees are planted when they are

    (a) fully grown   (b) in bloom   (c) tiny seeds

3. Seeds carried in rivers

    (a) shrink   (b) float   (c) fly

4. Seeds are *not* carried in

    (a) animals' fur   (b) the rain   (c) clouds

5. The passage suggests that it is

    (a) easy to plant a tree   (b) hard to plant a tree (c) the job of people to plant trees

Put the sentences in the correct order.

_____ Sometimes they fall on us.

_____ Have you ever wondered where trees come from?

_____ They are eaten by birds.

_____ Trees begin when they are tiny seeds.

Match the words with their meanings.

_____ 1. plant   (a) to rest on top of something, like water

_____ 2. tiny   (b) put here and there

_____ 3. float   (c) to put around

_____ 4. scattered   (d) to put in the ground to grow

_____ 5. spread   (e) very little

Write about it.

1. Write 2 sentences about the same subject. Use 1 of the words from "Match the words with their meanings."

2. Why do you think trees need to scatter their seeds? If all the seeds fell on the ground under the tree, do you think they could grow well? Why or why not?

3 Animal Lover

Ann loves animals. What do you think she wants to be?

Ann knows what she wants to be when she grows up — a **vet**. She loves being with animals and taking care of them.

Vets, or veterinarians, are animal doctors. They look after animals, not people. They take care of animals that are sick or hurt. Vets also help animals keep well by giving them **checkups**. They make sure the animal has no **pests**, such as fleas or **ticks**. They give them shots to keep them from getting sick.

Ann wants to go to school to be a vet when she grows up. It will take a long time. It is hard. But she will do it!

The passage is about

   (a) looking after people
   (b) looking after animals
   (c) looking after pests

Can you remember?

1. Ann wants to be
   (a) a zoo keeper
   (b) a vet
   (c) in a circus

2. Vets are

   (a) teachers   (b) doctors   (c) dentists

3. Vets look after

   (a) only sick animals   (b) only well animals   (c) both sick and well animals

4. Which is *not* a pest?

   (a) flea   (b) worm   (c) tick

5. Vets give animals shots to stop them from

   (a) getting sick   (b) having fleas   (c) eating too much

Put the sentences in the correct order.

_____ It will take a long time.

_____ Vets give animals shots.

_____ Ann knows what she is going to be.

_____ They look after animals instead of people.

Match the words with their meanings.

_____ 1. vet   (a) insects that make plants or animals sick

_____ 2. pests   (b) tiny insects that stick to animals and suck

_____ 3. checkup   their blood

_____ 4. ticks   (c) an exam where someone or something is looked over to see if everything is okay

                            (d) animal doctor

Write about it.

1. Write 2 sentences about the same subject. Use 1 of the words from "Match the words with their meanings."

2. Write about what you want to be when you grow up. If you do not know, write about what a parent or a friend does.

4 Cooking and Eating

What kind of food would you have cooked many years ago?

Cooking can be easy these days, but it wasn't so easy for the early **settlers**. They had to use mostly open fires. Food took a long time to cook. It all had to be **boiled** in one pot, because only one pot could fit over the fire. People ate a lot of stews, soups, and **chowders**.

They also liked to eat **wild** turkey and pigs. People say that they ate every part of the pig but its **squeal**!

Corn was easy to grow, so they had lots of it. They also had apples, nuts, maple sugar, and honey. These were easy to find or to make.

The passage is about

(a) the food we eat today

(b) cooking and eating in the early settlers' time

(c) how to cook a pig

Can you remember?

1. Long ago people cooked on

    (a) open fires   (b) gas stoves   (c) grilles

2. Most of their food was

    (a) baked   (b) boiled   (c) fried

3. They liked to eat

    (a) fried chicken   (b) hamburgers   (c) pigs

4. What food did they find in the woods?

    (a) honey   (b) corn   (c) potatoes

5. Which of their foods do we still eat today?

    (a) hot dogs   (b) stew   (c) pizza

Put the sentences in the correct order.

_____ They liked to eat wild turkey.

_____ Cooking can be easy these days.

_____ So they mainly ate stews, soups, and chowders.

_____ They had plenty of corn.

Match the words with their meanings.

_____ 1. settlers   (a) sharp, shrill cry or sound

_____ 2. boiled   (b) not tame

_____ 3. chowders   (c) cooked in boiling water

_____ 4. wild   (d) thick soups made of fish, clams, or vegetables

_____ 5. squeal   (e) people who travel to live in a new place

Write about it.

1. Write 2 sentences about the same subject. Use 1 of the words from "Match the words with their meanings."

2. Describe your favorite meal. Include details on how the food is prepared or cooked, and tell where you like to eat—at home, in a restaurant, at a picnic, or another place.

5   Johnny Appleseed

Do you know how Johnny Appleseed got his name?

Johnny Appleseed was the **nickname** for a man named John Chapman. He was born in New England around 1775. Johnny Appleseed loved planting and taking care of apple trees. He left his hometown near Boston and **traveled** west. He went to parts of the country where Native Americans lived. He became their friend. He ran into lots of wild animals and was very kind to them. People around the country began to hear about Johnny Appleseed. He kept on traveling, planting seeds, and taking care of apple trees wherever he went. People all over the country said he was a kind, **brave**, **unusual** man. He died in 1845.

The passage is about

  (a) how to plant an apple tree

  (b) a man who liked to plant apple trees

  (c) why we have so many apple trees

Can you remember?

1. Johnny planted apple seeds
   - (a) only in his hometown
   - (b) wherever he went
   - (c) where people asked him to

2. When he left home he traveled
   - (a) east
   - (b) west
   - (c) south

3. Johnny met
   - (a) Native Americans
   - (b) Pilgrims
   - (c) British

4. His real name was
   - (a) Johnny Appleseed
   - (b) John Smith
   - (c) John Chapman

5. He was born in
   - (a) New England
   - (b) the wilderness
   - (c) a Native American camp

Put the sentences in the correct order.

_____ He was known as a kind, brave man.

_____ Johnny Appleseed was his nickname.

_____ He left his hometown.

_____ He met lots of wild animals.

Match the words with their meanings.

_____ 1. traveled   (a) showing no fear

_____ 2. nickname   (b) not like other things or people

_____ 3. brave   (c) went on a trip

_____ 4. unusual   (d) not a real name

Write about it.

1. Write 2 sentences about the same subject. Use 1 of the words from "Match the words with their meanings."

2. The apple trees Johnny Appleseed planted made America more beautiful and gave people food. Describe what you could do to make your neighborhood or city more beautiful.

10

6 Susan B. Anthony

Susan B. Anthony was a brave woman. What did she do?

Susan B. Anthony was a brave woman who fought for people's **rights**. She lived over one hundred and fifty years ago. In those days women had to stay at home and do what men told them to do. But Susan B. Anthony was unusual. She spoke out. She spoke against **slavery**; she spoke for giving women the right to vote. She worked with other women. She gave **speeches**; she held meetings. She led the fight for the vote for women. Her work was a big help. After she died, women got the right to vote in 1920. Susan B. Anthony's picture was put on a one-dollar **coin** in 1979.

The passage is about

(a) a woman who helped other women

(b) our new coins

(c) slavery

Can you remember?

1. How long ago did Susan B. Anthony live?

(a) ten years

(b) one hundred and fifty years

(c) three hundred years

2. Anthony thought women should

   (a) stay at home   (b) have lots of   (c) have the same

                                    children   chances as men

3. She was also against

   (a) marrying   (b) slavery   (c) pets

4. She thought women should be able to

   (a) vote   (b) travel   (c) keep house

Put the sentences in the correct order.

_____ Susan B. Anthony spoke against slavery.

_____ She was unusual.

_____ She lived over one hundred and fifty years ago.

_____ Women got the right to vote in 1920.

Match the words with their meanings.

_____ 1. slavery   (a) being forced to work for someone

_____ 2. rights   (b) things that people should have by law

_____ 3. speeches   (c) talks given to people

_____ 4. coin   (d) money made of metal

Write about it.

1. Write 2 sentences about the same subject. Use 1 of the words from "Match the words with their meanings."

2. Susan B. Anthony was a powerful speaker. Write a speech about something that is important to you, or a speech that tries to persuade someone (such as a family member) to let you do something. Be sure to give good reasons to support your beliefs.

7 Driving in England

Have you ever heard of "cat's eyes"?

We drive on the right-hand side of the street here. But if you lived in England, you would drive a car or ride your bike on the left-hand side. England has many **narrow**, **curving** roads. "Cat's eyes" help people see the road and find the way. "Cat's eyes" are **bits** of glass. They are stuck into the middle of roads. At night, the lights of a car make the bits of glass shine, so it is easier to follow the road in the dark. The "cat's eyes" help you to see when a **bend** in the road is coming. "Cat's eyes" stop a lot of **accidents**.

The passage is about

    (a) cats   (b) driving in England   (c) renting a car

Can you remember?

1. In England people drive

    (a) on the left   (b) on the right   (c) down the middle of
                                                              the road

2. "Cat's eyes" are

    (a) part of a cat   (b) made of glass   (c) the lights of a car

3. What makes "cat's eyes" shine?

    (a) the sun   (b) the moon   (c) the lights of a car

4. Many English roads are

    (a) narrow   (b) straight   (c) bumpy

5. Having "cat's eyes" on the roads makes driving

    (a) safer   (b) less safe   (c) hard

Put the sentences in the correct order.

_____ They help you see when a bend is coming.

_____ "Cat's eyes" would help you find your way.

_____ You would ride your bike on the left-hand side.

_____ They are called this because the lights of cars make them shine at night.

Match the words with their meanings.

_____ 1. narrow   (a) something that you don't expect to happen

_____ 2. bend   (b) thin; not wide

_____ 3. curving   (c) small pieces

_____ 4. bits   (d) turn

_____ 5. accident   (e) not straight

Write about it.

1. Write 2 sentences about the same subject. Use 1 of the words from "Match the words with their meanings."

2. Because a cat's eyes shine in the dark, "cat's eyes" is a clever name for the road markers described in the selection. Make up a clever name for an ordinary item you use at home or school. Explain why it is a good name for the item.

8 Who Am I?

I have many **eyes**. My skin is brown. I have a jacket. What am I?

People all over the world like me. In fact, many people could not live without me.

When I am **young**, I am as small as a nut, but I grow to be as big as a baseball. I come in lots of shapes, but most of the time I'm shaped like an egg.

You can cook me many ways — bake, **fry**, or boil. You can use me to make soups, stews, **pancakes**, breads, and even cakes. However, the best way to eat me is all by myself. I taste very good, and I am good for you.

The passage is about

   (a) an egg   (b) a nut   (c) a potato

Can you remember?

1. Who likes this?

   (a) everyone   (b) just Americans   (c) just baseball players

2. When this thing is young, it's the size of
   (a) a seed   (b) a nut   (c) an orange

3. When this thing is grown, it is the size of
   (a) a football   (b) a basketball   (c) a baseball

4. How can you cook this?
   (a) fry and bake   (b) boil and bake   (c) many ways

5. The best way to eat this thing is
   (a) in cakes   (b) in stews   (c) alone

Put the sentences in the correct order.

_____ Everyone likes me.

_____ I am good for you.

_____ I am as big as a nut.

_____ You can use me to make soup.

Match the words with their meanings.

_____ 1. (potato) eyes   (a) cook in fat

_____ 2. fry   (b) flat cakes made of thin batter and cooked
               on both sides

_____ 3. young

_____ 4. pancakes   (c) spots on a potato where roots can grow

               (d) not old

Write about it.

1. Write 2 sentences about the same subject. Use 1 of the words from "Match the words with their meanings."

2. Write a "What Am I?" story. Describe something, but do not say what it is. Use lots of details. Then give your story to a friend to see if he or she can guess what you are describing.

16

9 Fingerprints

Do you know what makes your fingerprints?

If you look at the tips of your fingers and thumbs, you'll see lines on them. These lines make up your "fingerprints." They form a **pattern** that no one else in the world has. The pattern will be the same all your life.

When you put your fingers on something, no matter what it is, you leave your fingerprints on it. You can't see them unless you **sprinkle special** dust on them. Then they become very clear.

Fingerprints are useful because they can be used to find out who people are and where they have been.

To make a **copy** of your fingerprints, carefully press the tips of your fingers on an inked stamp pad and then on some paper. The paper should have the print on it.

The passage is about

   (a) finger painting   (b) printing letters   (c) fingerprints

Can you remember?

1. Fingerprints are
   (a) marks made by lines on your finger tips
   (b) dirty fingers
   (c) painted fingernails

2. Which is correct?
   (a) all fingerprints are the same
   (b) all fingerprints are different
   (c) you have the same fingerprints as your parents

3. To see fingerprints, cover them with
   (a) water
   (b) paint
   (c) special dust

4. Which is *not* correct? Fingerprints are useful because they can tell
   (a) who people are
   (b) where people have been
   (c) how old people are

5. Who would find fingerprints the most useful?
   (a) a doctor
   (b) a police officer
   (c) a printer

Put the sentences in the correct order.

_____ Fingerprints are useful.

_____ You leave your fingerprints on it.

_____ You'll see lines on them.

_____ Put some ink on your fingers.

Match the words with their meanings.

_____ 1. special   (a) drop little bits of something

_____ 2. pattern   (b) form, design

_____ 3. copy   (c) something that isn't the way it usually is; something different

_____ 4. sprinkle

           (d) something just like something else

Write about it.

1. Write 2 sentences about the same subject. Use 1 of the words from "Match the words with their meanings."

2. No one else has the same fingerprints as you. Write about something else that makes you different and special.

18

10 I Am Important!

Sometimes I can't be seen or touched. Sometimes I can be **poured**. Sometimes I'm as hard as stone. What am I?

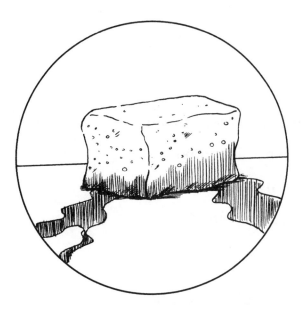

You use me every day. In fact, you could not live without me. I am found all over the earth. Most of the time you see me as a **liquid**, but I can also be a **solid** or a gas — like ice or snow, or steam. I am part of all living things. Without me, living things would die.

I can also be used in millions of ways to make things work better, to cool things, to clean things, and to make heat and **power**.

The passage is about

   (a) air   (b) water   (c) gold

Can you remember?

1. This thing
   (a) is always changing   (b) will not change   (c) cannot change

2. What does *not* make it change?
   (a) heat   (b) cold   (c) the wind

3. When it's very cold this becomes

    (a) soft   (b) hard   (c) smooth

4. When it's very hot this

    (a) boils   (b) freezes   (c) becomes soft

5. You *cannot*

    (a) wash with it   (b) walk in it   (c) sharpen a pencil
                                                with it

Put the sentences in the correct order.

_____ I can be used for heat and power.

_____ I am part of all living things.

_____ Sometimes I can be poured.

_____ I'm used every day.

Match the words with their meanings.

_____ 1. liquid   (a) something that is thick and hard; not a liquid

_____ 2. poured   (b) force that makes something work

_____ 3. solid   (c) something that flows like water

_____ 4. power   (d) let something flow out

Write about it.

1. Write 2 sentences about the same subject. Use 1 of the words from "Match the words with their meanings."

2. Did you guess that the story was about water? Tell about 4 ways you use water in your life. Discuss what you would do if your water supply were very limited. For example, if you tell about washing dishes, how would you clean dishes with little or no water?

11 Kittens

Have you ever seen new-born kittens? Think about what they are like.

Kittens can't hear until they are a few days old. They can't see for about ten days. And they don't get their first teeth until they are about two months old.

The kitten's fur is thin at first. But it has the same color and pattern that it will have when it gets thicker.

Kittens sleep a lot until they are about a month old. Then they are ready to **explore** their world and to have fun. They learn to wash themselves, **hunt**, and climb trees by watching their mother. When it is dark, their **whiskers** help them tell what things are.

By ten weeks, a kitten is ready to leave its mother. It may be ready for you to have as a pet.

The passage is about

   (a) how to look after   (b) what kittens are   (c) why kittens are
       a kitten   like   different colors

Can you remember?

1. When kittens are born they
   (a) have no fur   (b) can't see   (c) have no claws

2. Kittens get their first teeth when they are
   (a) two days old   (b) two weeks old   (c) two months old

3. Their first fur is
   (a) white   (b) thin   (c) very thick

4. A cat's whiskers are used to
   (a) eat   (b) scratch   (c) find objects in
                                                     the dark

5. A kitten is ready to leave its mother in
   (a) four weeks   (b) eight weeks   (c) ten weeks

Put the sentences in the correct order.

_____ Kittens can't hear until they are a few days old.

_____ Kittens sleep a lot until they are about a month old.

_____ The fur has the same color and pattern it will have when it gets thicker.

_____ It is perhaps ready for you to have as a pet.

Match the words with their meanings.

_____ 1. explore   (a) hairs growing on the sides of the face or on

_____ 2. whiskers   the chin

_____ 3. hunt   (b) look around; search through

                                 (c) to look for an animal to kill for food

Write about it.

1. Write 2 sentences about the same subject. Use 1 of the words from "Match the words with their meanings."

2. Would you like to have a kitten? Tell why or why not.

12   A Sea Monster?

What did Susan meet under water? Was it a sea monster?

Yes ☐   No ☐

Susan was swimming under water when something came near her. It had a round middle with eight long arms sticking out of it. Each arm had rows of little cups that could hold things tightly. In its middle was a mouth with two **beaks** as sharp as knife **blades**.

In the past, many sailors had been afraid of this animal. But Susan was not afraid. She was a **scientist** learning about the **octopus**. She knew that it eats crabs and other small shellfish from the bottom of the sea. She knew that some octopuses give off lots of ink when they feel in danger. This makes a screen so their enemies can't see them slip away. Susan hoped this would not happen because she wanted to watch the octopus so she could learn more about it.

The passage is about

   (a) sea monsters   (b) an octopus   (c) how to swim under
                                                          water

23

Can you remember?

1. How many arms did the creature have
   (a) four (b) eight (c) eighteen

2. What did the arms have on them?
   (a) cups (b) sharp spikes (c) fingers

3. What did its mouth have?
   (a) a long tongue (b) sharp teeth (c) sharp beaks

4. In the past, sailors thought an octopus was
   (a) good to eat (b) nice to have as a pet (c) something to be afraid of

5. Susan was
   (a) doing her job (b) having fun (c) swimming in a race

Put the sentences in the correct order.

_____ In the past, sailors had been afraid.

_____ Susan was swimming under the water.

_____ Was it a sea monster?

_____ She was a scientist learning more about how it lives.

Match the words with their meanings.

_____ 1. beak

_____ 2. scientist

_____ 3. octopus

_____ 4. blade

(a) someone who knows a lot about science, the way things in the world are and why

(b) the bill of an animal, sometimes sharp

(c) a small, eight-armed animal that lives in the sea

(d) the cutting part of something

Write about it.

1. Write 2 sentences about the same subject. Use 1 of the words from "Match the words with their meanings."

2. Make up a story about a monster. Make the monster as strange and scary as you can.

24

13 Seeing Stars

Did you know that the sun is a star?

The best time to see stars is on a **clear** night when there is no moon. Stars make their own light. They shine all the time, day and night. There's only one star you can see in the day. That is the sun.

The sun is a ball of hot, **glowing gas**. Its light is so bright that in the day it hides the light of the other stars so we can't see them.

The sun is not the biggest and brightest star. But it looks as if it is because it is **closer** to the earth than the other stars. The farther away a star is from us, the less bright it looks and the harder it is to see. There are billions of stars in the world. They are all different sizes, shapes, colors, and ages.

The passage is about

   (a) how to catch a star   (b) the stars   (c) how the sun keeps us warm

Can you remember?

1. The best time to see stars is when
   - (a) the moon is out
   - (b) there is no moon
   - (c) the sun is shining

2. The sun is made of
   - (a) hot gas
   - (b) cold gas
   - (c) hot rock

3. Which is correct? The sun is
   - (a) the biggest star
   - (b) the brightest star
   - (c) the star closest to earth

4. The farther a star is from earth
   - (a) the brighter it shines
   - (b) the less chance we have of seeing it
   - (c) the hotter it is

5. Stars shine
   - (a) only in the daytime
   - (b) only at night
   - (c) all the time

Put the sentences in the correct order

_____ The sun is a ball of hot, glowing gas.

_____ Did you know the sun is a star?

_____ The sun is not the biggest and brightest star.

_____ The best time to look at stars is on a clear night.

Match the words with their meanings.

_____ 1. clear   (a) nearer

_____ 2. glowing   (b) bright, with no clouds; nothing in the way

_____ 3. closer   (c) shining brightly

_____ 4. gas   (d) something, like air, that has no shape and tends to expand

Write about it.

1. Write 2 sentences about the same subject. Use 1 of the words from "Match the words with their meanings."

2. The story describes the sun. Give 3 ways that the sun helps all living things to survive.

14　The Lazy Cat

This bird knew that it was not safe to go into the cat's **den**.

Toby was a wild cat who lived in a city park. He was a very lazy cat. He also liked to eat. Even when it was cold and snowy, he knew how to get his meals without ever leaving where he slept. He would stay in his **snug** den in the **shrubs**.

He pretended to be sick. He would **moan** and groan loudly so the birds and mice could hear him. When they came to look around, he would jump on them and eat them.

One winter day a sparrow heard the cat moaning and asked, "What is the matter?"

"I'm so sick," replied the cat. "Can you come into my den and help me?"

The little bird looked at the snow and saw the footprints. She turned around and went on her way.

The passage is about

(a) a smart cat and a foolish bird

(b) a foolish cat and a smart bird

(c) a smart cat and a smart bird

Can you remember?

1. Toby lived in
   (a) a back yard   (b) the woods   (c) a park

2. Toby liked to
   (a) lie in the sun   (b) eat   (c) chat with the animals

3. When it was cold, Toby
   (a) stopped eating   (b) found shelter in a house   (c) stayed in his den

4. The birds and mice
   (a) were curious about the cat   (b) were afraid of the cat   (c) did errands for the cat

5. The sparrow did not go into the cat's den because she
   (a) saw bones   (b) was afraid of the cat   (c) saw footprints that went only into the den

Put the sentences in the correct order.

_____ A sparrow heard the cat moaning.

_____ Toby also liked to eat.

_____ Toby was a wild cat.

_____ The little bird turned around.

Match the words with their meanings.

_____ 1. moan   (a) a place for wild animals to live or rest

_____ 2. snug   (b) bushes

_____ 3. shrubs   (c) cozy, warm

_____ 4. den   (d) to make a long, low sound of sadness or pain

Write about it.

1. Write 2 sentences about the same subject. Use 1 of the words from "Match the words with their meanings."

2. Imagine that you were the smart bird who got away from the crafty cat. Write what you would tell your friends about your meeting with the cat.

15   The Dodo Bird

Have you ever seen one? Could you have?

The dodo was an **odd** bird. Dodos lived on an **island** in the Indian Ocean. They were last seen around 1670. They were related to pigeons, but they could not fly. They were a little bit bigger than a turkey, with a big blackish bill, which ended in a large, **horny** hook. Dodos liked to live in woods and would lay one large white egg on a pile of grass. People think the dodos died out because of the **hogs** the settlers brought with them. The hogs ate the dodos' eggs and their babies.

The name *dodo* means "silly" in **Portuguese**. The settlers named the birds this. Do you think it was a good name?

The passage is about

   (a) keeping a dodo as a pet   (b) what happened to dodos   (c) how to catch a dodo

Can you remember?

1. Dodos were related to

   (a) pigeons   (b) ducks   (c) turkeys

2. The settlers came from
   (a) the United States   (b) India   (c) Portugal

3. Dodo means
   (a) quiet   (b) silly   (c) sad

4. The dodo lived
   (a) in the woods   (b) in the desert   (c) on an island

5. Dodos died because
   (a) their eggs and   (b) they became   (c) they were attacked
       babies were eaten   very sick   by the settlers

Put the sentences in the correct order.

_____ The hogs ate the dodos' eggs.

_____ Do you think *dodo* was a good name?

_____ They were a little bit bigger than a turkey.

_____ They lived on an island.

Match the words with their meanings.

_____ 1. odd   (a) like or made of horn, which is something hard

_____ 2. horny   and bony

_____ 3. Portuguese   (b) full-grown pigs

_____ 4. hogs   (c) strange

_____ 5. island   (d) land with water all around it

                       (e) what people who live in Portugal speak

Write about it.

1. Write 2 sentences about the same subject. Use 1 of the words from "Match the words with their meanings."

2. As you learned from the selection, dodos became extinct (died out). Find out about another animal in danger of becoming extinct, such as the panda. Write whether you think people should try to save this animal from dying out.

16 Cat Care

Thinking of getting a cat for a pet? Here are some tips for looking after her.
SLEEPING:

We all like a warm, snug place to sleep. Cats do, too. Get a box and fill it with soft rags — like a bit of old blanket or sweater. Put the box in a quiet place.

EATING:

Give your cat its own dish. Feed it twice a day — in the morning and at night. You can get cat food at the **market**. Keep a dish of **fresh** water on the floor. Cats need water just like dogs.

KEEPING CLEAN:

Cats wash themselves, but you should brush your cat's coat. Make a **litter** box. Take a pan or box and fill it with sand or cat litter. To **train** her to use it, take her to it after she eats. She will learn to go to it on her own.

The passage is about

   (a) why cats make   (b) how to look after   (c) how to train a cat
        good pets   a cat

Can you remember?

1. What should you put in your cat's bed?

    (a) a pillow   (b) straw   (c) soft rags

2. How many times a day should a cat eat?

    (a) one   (b) two   (c) three

3. What should you leave on the floor for your cat?

    (a) milk   (b) water   (c) food

4. A litter box has

    (a) sand   (b) soil   (c) stones

5. To keep your cat clean, you should

    (a) wash it   (b) brush it   (c) keep it inside

Put the sentences in the correct order.

_____ You can get cat food at the market.

_____ We all like a warm, cozy place to sleep.

_____ Make sure you give your cat its own dish.

_____ Make a litter box.

Match the words with their meanings.

_____ 1. litter   (a) teach

_____ 2. market   (b) store

_____ 3. fresh   (c) new

_____ 4. train   (d) something like sand or pebbles that cats use
                              for a toilet

Write about it.

1. Write 2 sentences about the same subject. Use 1 of the words from "Match the words with their meanings."

2. Imagine that someone has told you that you can't have a pet because you won't know how to care for it. Using what you have learned from this selection, explain why you think you could take good care of an animal.

17 An Odd Spider

What is odd about this spider?

Most spiders live on land, but this spider is different. It spends most of its time under water. How does it breathe? It breathes by making a tent full of air bubbles under water.

First it **spins** a **web** in the shape of a bell. Then it **fixes** it to plants under the water. Next it swims up to the top of the water and **traps** a tiny bubble of air with its hairy back legs. It **drags** the bubble to its web. It does this many times until its home is full of air. Then it sits nice and snug in its web and feeds on tiny fish and other water animals.

The passage is about a spider that

    (a) can't spin a web   (b) lives under water   (c) lives in plants

Can you remember?

1. Most spiders

    (a) fly   (b) live on land   (c) live under water

2. How does the spider live under water?

    (a) it holds its breath   (b) it lives in air   (c) it lives under a rock

                                                          bubbles

3. This spider

    (a) can spin a web   (b) can't spin a web   (c) spins a web of gold

                                                           thread

4. The spider catches an air bubble with its

    (a) mouth   (b) front legs   (c) back legs

5. The name of this spider must be

    (a) tree spider   (b) plant spider   (c) water spider

Put the sentences in the correct order.

_____ It traps an air bubble.

_____ It fixes the web to plants.

_____ It drags the air bubble to its web.

_____ It spins a web.

Match the words with their meanings.

_____ 1. fixes   (a) pulls, sometimes something heavy or big

_____ 2. spins   (b) joins one thing to another

_____ 3. web   (c) a spider's home made of threads it makes

_____ 4. drags   (d) catches

_____ 5. traps   (e) pulls and twists to make a thread

Write about it.

1. Write 2 sentences about the same subject. Use 1 of the words from "Match the words with their meanings."

2. Write a story about another creature with unusual behavior. You can either find out about a real animal, or make up a fictional story.

18 How Odd

Do you live on the odd or the even side of the street?

It was Jenny's first day on her new job — **delivering** the mail. She had no **trouble** finding the right house numbers. Look at the numbers of the houses on your street and you may see why.

On one side the numbers end with 1, 3, 5, 7, or 9. On the other side the numbers end with 2, 4, 6, 8, or 0. These are called the ODD and EVEN sides of the street.

The numbers take turns back and forth across the street: odd — even — odd — even.

① 2 ③ 4 ⑤ 6 ⑦ 8 ⑨ 10 ⑪ 12 ⑬ 14 ⑮ 16 ⑰ 18 ⑲

On this page, the numbers with the circles are ODD. The numbers with the squares are EVEN.

If a number with more than one **digit** (like 187) ends in an odd number, it's called — yes — an odd number. If a number with more than one digit (like 256) ends in an even number — you've got it — it's called an even number.

What's the number of your house? Is it odd or even?

The passage is about

    (a) strange numbers   (b) a wrong number   (c) odd and even numbers

Can you remember?

1. Which of these is an odd number

    (a) 2   (b) 5   (c) 8

2. 1, 2, 3, 4, 5 are

    (a) all odd numbers   (b) all even numbers   (c) both odd and even
                                                        numbers

3. The even number is

    (a) 7   (b) 8   (c) 9

4. All the numbers with squares are

    (a) odd   (b) even   (c) both odd and even

5. If the number of your house ends in an odd number it

    (a) is on the odd side   (b) is on the even side   (c) can be on either side

Put the sentences in the correct order.

_____ It was Jenny's first day on her new job.

_____ The numbers take turns back and forth across the street.

_____ On one side the numbers end with 1, 3, 5, 7, or 9.

_____ Is the number of your house odd or even?

Match the words with their meanings.

_____ 1. digit   (a) taking something to a person or place

_____ 2. delivering   (b) any number from 0-9

_____ 3. trouble   (c) difficulty, something that is hard

Write about it.

1. Write 2 sentences about the same subject. Use 1 of the words from "Match the words with their meanings."

2. This story mentions a mail carrier. Would you like to have this job? Tell why or why not.

19 Remembering Numbers

How many numbers can you add up at one time?

Andy and his 7 friends went on the bus to the ball game. The **fare** was 25 cents each. The tickets to get into the game cost $2.00.

While they were watching the game, the kids got 5 boxes of popcorn, 8 ice cream cones, 3 hamburgers, and 4 hot dogs. The popcorn cost $1.00; the ice creams cost 50 cents; the hamburgers cost $1.50; and the hot dogs cost $1.50.

The game was great, but 3 players were **injured**. The red team beat the blue team by 6 points.

The bus back was **crowded** and slow. It was 6 o'clock before they got home.

The passage is about

   (a) the zoo   (b) the beach   (c) a ball game

Can you remember?

1. How many friends went to the ball game with Andy?

   (a) 3   (b) 5   (c) 7

2. How many hot dogs did they get?

   (a) 3   (b) 4   (c) 5

3. What did they all have?

   (a) an ice cream cone   (b) a hot dog   (c) a hamburger

4. The red team beat the blue team by

   (a) 2 points   (b) 4 points   (c) 6 points

5. When did they get home?

   (a) 3 o'clock   (b) 6 o'clock   (c) 9 o'clock

Put the sentences in the correct order.

_____ The game was great.

_____ The tickets to get into the game cost $2.00.

_____ The kids got 5 boxes of popcorn.

_____ The bus was crowded and slow going home.

Match the words with their meanings.

_____ 1. fare   (a) filled with a lot of people

_____ 2. injured   (b) hurt

_____ 3. crowded   (c) money you pay to go on the train, bus, or
                                   plane

Write about it.

1. Write 2 sentences about the same subject. Use 1 of the words from "Match the words with their meanings."

2. The story tells about a baseball game. Write about your favorite game and tell why you like it.

20 Cookies for Sale

A **chart** can tell a story.

Lots of kids in Hampton were selling cookies. Look at the chart to see who sold the most and to answer the questions **below**.

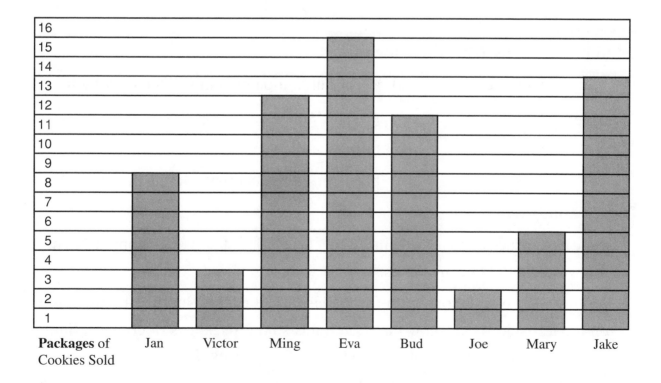

	Jan	Victor	Ming	Eva	Bud	Joe	Mary	Jake
16								
15				■				
14				■				
13				■				■
12			■	■				■
11			■	■	■			■
10			■	■	■			■
9			■	■	■			■
8	■		■	■	■			■
7	■		■	■	■			■
6	■		■	■	■			■
5	■		■	■	■		■	■
4	■		■	■	■		■	■
3	■	■	■	■	■		■	■
2	■	■	■	■	■	■	■	■
1	■	■	■	■	■	■	■	■

Packages of
Cookies Sold

39

The chart is about

    (a) how many cookies   (b) how to sell cookies   (c) the kinds of cookies

          everyone sold   people sold

Can you remember?

1. Who sold the most cookies?

    (a) Jake   (b) Eva   (c) Ming

2. Who sold *next* to the most?

    (a) Jan   (b) Ming   (c) Jake

3. Who sold the smallest number of cookies?

    (a) Victor   (b) Joe   (c) Mary

4. Who sold eleven packages of cookies?

    (a) Bud   (b) Ming   (c) Jan

5. How many packets did Mary sell?

    (a) 4   (b) 5   (c) 12

Begin with the person who sold the *smallest* number of cookies, and list the kids in order of the number of packages of cookies they sold.

_____ Jan   _____ Joe

_____ Mary   _____ Victor

Match the words with their meanings.

_____ 1. packages   (a) a list that compares things; an easy way to

_____ 2. chart   give facts

_____ 3. below   (b) underneath

                         (c) boxes or cases that have things in them

Write about it.

1. Write 2 sentences about the same subject. Use 1 of the words from "Match the words with their meanings."

2. Make a chart like the one in the story. Use lined paper. Number the lines 1–8 on the left side. Then show that Loren has sold 6 packages of cookies, Sam has sold 2 packages, and Kalima has sold 5 packages. If you wish, use a different-colored crayon or pencil for each student.

21   The Great Rain

Why did the animals go on this boat two-by-two?

In the story from the Old Testament,* God called Noah to him. "The people of the earth are **wicked**. They will die in a **flood**. You are a good man. I want you to make a boat — an **ark**. When it is ready, go out and find two of every animal on earth. Then put them in the boat."

Noah called his three sons, and they made the boat. Everyone laughed and said they were **foolish**. Then they got 2 monkeys, 2 elephants, 2 snakes, 2 ants, and 2 of every other animal. They went onto the boat two-by-two.

When they were all on the boat, God made it rain. It rained for 40 days and 40 nights. Only those on the boat were saved.

The passage is about

    (a) what to do on
           a rainy day

    (b) how to make
           a boat

    (c) how Noah and the
           animals were saved

* Holy writings of the Christian and Jewish religions.

Can you remember?

1. Noah

   (a) was a good man   (b) liked animals   (c) was a fisherman

2. How many of each animal did God tell him to get?

   (a) 1   (b) 2   (c) 3

3. How many sons did he have?

   (a) 2   (b) 3   (c) 5

4. When did it begin to rain?

   (a) *before* they got   (b) *after* they got   (c) as they were getting

      on the boat   on the boat   on the boat

5. How many days and nights did it rain?

   (a) 2   (b) 4   (c) 40

Put the sentences in the correct order.

_____ They went into the boat two at a time.

_____ God called Noah to him.

_____ Noah called his three sons.

_____ Only the people and animals on the boat were saved.

Match the words with their meanings.

_____ 1. wicked   (a) water that spreads all over a place that's

_____ 2. flood   usually dry

_____ 3. ark   (b) very, very bad; evil;

_____ 4. foolish   (c) a boat written about in the Bible that kept

                       animals and people safe

                   (d) not wise

Write about it.

1. Write 2 sentences about the same subject. Use 1 of the words from "Match the words with their meanings."

2. Imagine that a flood is coming, but you have enough time to escape. You can choose 5 things to take with you. Tell what things you would take and why they are important to you.

22 The Ostrich Is a Silly bird

The ostrich is a **silly** bird
With **scarcely** any **mind**.
He often runs so very fast,
He leaves himself behind.

And when he gets there, has to stand
And **hang about** till night,
Without a blessed thing to do
Until he comes in sight.

– Mary E. Wilkins Freeman

The poem says that the ostrich is

   (a) fast   (b) slow   (c) large

Can you remember?

1. When the ostrich runs he

   (a) beats everyone   (b) trips over himself   (c) leaves himself behind

2. He has to wait for

   (a) several hours   (b) night time   (c) the next day

3. While he is waiting he
   - (a) stands
   - (b) lies down
   - (c) buries his head in the sand

4. The ostrich is
   - (a) funny
   - (b) silly
   - (c) smart

5. The poem is meant to
   - (a) be funny
   - (b) be serious
   - (c) tell you all about ostriches

Put the sentences in the correct order.

_____ without a blessed thing to do

_____ Until he comes in sight

_____ He leaves himself behind.

_____ The ostrich is a silly bird.

Match the words with their meanings.

_____ 1. silly   (a) very little

_____ 2. scarcely   (b) brains

_____ 3. mind   (c) foolish

_____ 4. hang about   (d) stay around

Write about it.

1. Write 2 sentences about the same subject. Use 1 of the words from "Match the words with their meanings."

2. Write a poem or the words to a song about an animal you like.

23 The Fox and the Crow

This story has something to say. It has a lesson called a **moral**.

A fox saw that a crow had a large bit of cheese in its beak.

"I bet that's **tasty**," he said to himself. "That would do me nicely for dinner. But how can I get it?"

Soon he had an idea. "My you're good looking," he told the crow, "and you sing so prettily. Please sing to me so I can hear your lovely voice."

This pleased the crow very much. He **puffed** himself up and opened his beak wide so he could sing loudly. The cheese fell to the ground and the fox **pounced** on it.

"Oh dear, oh dear," said the crow. "How silly I was to listen to that **flatterer**."

The passage is about

(a) how a fox tricked a crow

(b) how a crow tricked a fox

(c) how a fox and crow fought over a piece of cheese

Can you remember?

1. The crow had the cheese in his
   (a) claws   (b) beak   (c) nest

2. The fox wanted the cheese for
   (a) breakfast   (b) lunch   (c) dinner

3. The fox did *not* tell the crow he
   (a) was good looking   (b) had lovely feathers (c) sang well

4. The fox won the cheese by
   (a) talking to the crow   (b) hitting the crow   (c) eating the crow

5. The lesson of the story is
   (a) don't eat cheese   (b) don't listen to   (c) don't listen to people
                             foxes   who praise you too
                                                  much

Put the sentences in the correct order.

_____ "Oh dear, oh dear," said the crow.

_____ This pleased the crow very much.

_____ A fox saw that a crow had some cheese in his beak.

_____ Soon the fox thought of something.

Match the words with their meanings.

_____ 1. tasty   (a) jumped on quickly

_____ 2. puffed (up) (b) made bigger by filling with air

_____ 3. pounced   (c) good to eat, good-tasting

_____ 4. flatterer   (d) someone who gives too much praise and

_____ 5. moral   really doesn't mean it

                          (e) a lesson one can learn from a story

Write about it.

1. Write 2 sentences about the same subject. Use 1 of the words from "Match the words with their meanings."

2. Do you feel sorry for the crow? Why or why not?

24 A Story with a Point

Everyone was afraid of it. It had lived on the earth since people could remember.

It was the most terrible **creature**. It looked like a **giant**. It moved like a giant. But what it was made of no one knew. All they did know what that it liked to fight. It had killed many people, but no one was able to kill it.

The story was that long ago it had saved the Goddess of Time from death. To show her thanks she had given it **everlasting** life. She had taken it by the neck and dipped it in a magic **mixture**. This made a skin all over it that nothing could break.

When Alex heard this story, he knew how he could kill the creature. He took a sharp needle. When it was lying down fast asleep he **pricked** the creature and it bled to death.

Where did he prick the creature?

The passage is about

(a) how a giant
killed people

(b) how a person
killed a giant

(c) how a goddess
killed a giant

Can you remember?

1. The creature looked like

    (a) a dragon   (b) a monster   (c) a giant

2. The creature liked to

    (a) eat   (b) fight   (c) sleep

3. The creature was covered with

    (a) magic skin   (b) a thick cloth   (c) a hard metal

4. What did Alex kill the creature with?

    (a) a gun   (b) a knife   (c) a needle

5. Alex pricked the creature in its

    (a) arm   (b) chest   (c) neck

Put the sentences in the correct order.

_____ It was the most terrible creature.

_____ To show her thanks she had given it everlasting life.

_____ Alex knew how he could kill the creature.

_____ Everyone was afraid of the creature.

Match the words with their meanings.

_____ 1. creature   (a) an animal or a person

_____ 2. pricked   (b) things that are put together

_____ 3. everlasting   (c) stuck something sharp or pointed into

_____ 4. mixture   something else

_____ 5. giant   (d) never ending

                      (e) a very big person who is not real

Write about it.

1. Write 2 sentences about the same subject. Use 1 of the words from "Match the words with their meanings."

2. This story tells about a giant. Write a story about a person or group of people who are very small. Describe how they live, where they sleep, what they eat, and so on.

25 A Trip to the Store

Who spent more money at the store, Joe or Jan?

Joe had $50 to spend. Jan had $50 to spend. They went to the **local** department store to buy some things they had wanted for a long time.

First they went to the sporting goods **section**. Joe bought a $15 football and Jan got a bat and baseball for $12. Next they went to clothing. Joe tried on a light blue jacket for $40, but it cost too much money. He bought a $20 shirt instead. Jan bought a bright red sweater for $25. **Finally** they **shared** the cost of a model rocket set, which cost $16. They planned to set up a toy space station.

The passage is about

   (a) a shopping trip   (b) a clothing store   (c) two friends

Can you remember?

1. How much did Joe have to spend?

   (a) $15   (b) $50   (c) $16

2. Which part of the store did they go to first?

    (a) clothing   (b) books   (c) sporting goods

3. Joe bought

    (a) a football   (b) a baseball   (c) a jacket

4. Jan bought

    (a) a football   (b) a baseball   (c) a dress

5. They both bought

    (a) a football   (b) a jacket   (c) a rocket set

Put the sentences in the correct order.

_____ They went to the store.

_____ Jan had $50 to spend.

_____ They planned to set up a toy space station.

_____ Joe tried on a jacket.

Match the words with their meanings.

_____ 1. local   (a) did, had or used with someone else

_____ 2. section   (b) at last

_____ 3. shared   (c) nearby; in your neighborhood

_____ 4. finally   (d) part of something

Write about it.

1. Write 2 sentences about the same subject. Use 1 of the words from "Match the words with their meanings."

2. Write about 3 things you would buy if you had some money to spend. Why do you want these things?

26 A Colorful Story

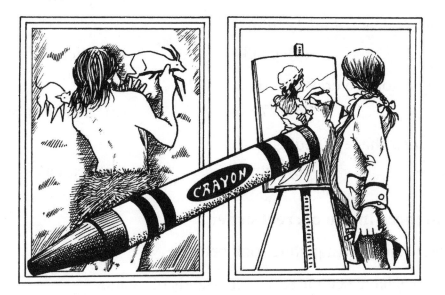

Color can make a picture look better. You can use paint, but crayons are easier.

Crayons have been used for thousands of years. In the **Stone Age,** people used coloring sticks to make pictures on cave walls. Later, **artists** used coloring sticks of chalk. The name crayon comes from a French word meaning "pencil."

Today crayons are made by mixing hot wax with colored **powder**. They come in every color you can think of — and more. Here are just a few of the shades of red: pink, rose, scarlet, **crimson**, ruby, and wine. Can you think of others?

The passage is about

    (a) candles   (b) crayons   (c) soap

Can you remember?

1. People in the Stone Age used colored sticks to draw on

    (a) stone   (b) paper   (c) cave walls

2. *Crayon* comes from the French word meaning

    (a) chalk   (b) color   (c) pencil

3. Today our crayons are made from

    (a) wax   (b) chalk   (c) sticks

4. How many colors do crayons come in today?

    (a) 7   (b) 27   (c) a great many

5. Which is *not* a shade of red?

    (a) rose   (b) lemon   (c) scarlet

Put the sentences in the correct order.

_____ Color can make a picture look better.

_____ Crayons have been used for thousands of years.

_____ How many other crayon colors can you think of?

_____ Artists used coloring sticks of chalk.

Match the words with their meanings.

_____ 1. Stone Age   (a) something made by pounding or crushing

_____ 2. artists   (b) people who are very good at drawing, painting, sculpture, music, writing, or other kinds of art

_____ 3. powder

_____ 4. crimson

    (c) the oldest time in which human beings are known to have lived

    (d) bright red; the color of blood

Write about it.

1. Write 2 sentences about the same subject. Use 1 of the words from "Match the words with their meanings."

2. What is your favorite color? Describe some things you like that are in that color, or tell how the color makes you feel.

27 Making Your Own Puppet

You don't need much to make a **puppet**. In fact, puppets can be made very **cheaply** — if you keep your eyes open and do a little work.

Look out for things with odd shapes or things you think will make good puppet parts. When you're out walking, look for strange-shaped stones, bits of wood and sticks, pine cones, nuts or leaves, or some shells. Then from around the house pick up a button or two, some **scraps** of colored paper and cloth, some bottle tops, and some empty cans or **cartons**. Get some **glue**. And then put your mind to work!

Here are some puppets you can copy if you run out of ideas.

  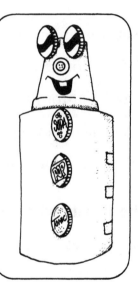

string	pine cone	cardboard
acorns	berries	paper cup
shell	matchstick	bottle tops
a stone	thread spool	can
red paper	button	button
wood	nails	white paper

The passage is about how to make something to

(a) wear   (b) eat   (c) use

Can you remember?

1. You can make a puppet cheaply if you
   - (a) get things at the supermarket
   - (b) look for old ones
   - (c) keep your eyes open and do a little work

2. The best things to make puppets from are
   - (a) big
   - (b) small
   - (c) oddly shaped

3. To make a good puppet, you need to
   - (a) use your mind
   - (b) be an artist
   - (c) be a fast worker

4. What would *not* make good eyes?
   - (a) bottle tops
   - (b) berries
   - (c) pine cones

5. What would make good hair?
   - (a) a thread spool
   - (b) string
   - (c) buttons

Put the sentences in the correct order.

_____ When you're outside look for strange-shaped stones.

_____ Look out for things with odd shapes.

_____ You can make a puppet cheaply.

_____ Then put your mind to work!

Match the words with their meanings.

_____ 1. puppet   (a) small bits, odds and ends

_____ 2. cheaply   (b) not costing much

_____ 3. scraps   (c) something used to stick things together

_____ 4. cartons   (d) a doll moved by hand

_____ 5. glue   (e) boxes

Write about it.

1. Write 2 sentences about the same subject. Use 1 of the words from "Match the words with their meanings."

2. Describe a puppet you could make from things in your home, classroom, or neighborhood. If you wish, draw a picture of your puppet to go along with your description.